To: My Single Friends

ALLIE SHIRLEY

Copyright © 2019 Author Allie Shirley
All rights reserved.
ISBN: 9781674439907

TO: MY SINGLE FRIENDS

DEDICATION

This devotional is dedicated to my Comforter and my Sustainer, Jesus Christ who has carried me through the darkest valleys and rejoiced over me on the highest mountain tops.

TO: MY SINGLE FRIENDS

TO: MY SINGLE FRIENDS

CONTENTS:

Dedication
Day 1: Made In His Image
Day 2: Did You Hear God Say That?
Day 3: No Limit
Day 4: Stop Frantically Searching
Day 5: Faith
Day 6: Nothing Is Wasted
Day 7: High Standards
Day 8: God Hears You
Day 9: How To Wrestle Well
Day 10: Rejection
Day 11: Surrender
Day 12: Waiting Well
Day 13: This Is Love
Day 14: Know Your Worth
Day 15: In Seconds
Day 16: Yes Lord
Day 17: Chase Your Dreams Now
Day 18: "If __ Happens.."
Day 19: Unshakeable Faith
Day 20: Settling? No Way!
Day 21: Waiting On Him
Day 22: Immeasurably More
Day 23: Distraction
Day 24: Believe
Day 25: No Quick Miracles
Day 26: Community Matters
Day 27: Let's Be Honest
Day 28: How Much More
Day 29: What I've Learned
Day 30: I'll Wait Declaration
A Prayer for the Holidays
Two Options
Another Single Holiday
Tis The Season
About The Author

TO: MY SINGLE FRIENDS

TO: MY SINGLE FRIENDS

DAY 1: MADE IN HIS IMAGE

Romans 8:28-31

"And we know that in all things God works for the good of those who love him, who have been called according to his purpose. For those God foreknew he also predestined to be conformed to the image of his Son, that he might be the firstborn among many brothers and sisters. And those he predestined, he also called; those he called, he also justified; those he justified, he also glorified." What, then, shall we say in response to these things? If God is for us, who can be against us?"

Single Friends,

Here's the thing, you are made in the image of God; therefore, you have a part to play in His story. The story where we proclaim His glory and tell as many people as we can about His unending love. A husband or a wife is an added bonus to the story He is writing. Your purpose doesn't come when he or she shows up. Your purpose is right now. YOU get to decide whether you waste that time wishing things were different or making the most of the days God has given you. Don't get me wrong do I wish that person was by my side through all the big and small moments? Absolutely.

But what if I had said to God "well I'll go do all you've called me to do when that person comes but until then I'm just going to wait." NO! If I had done that, I would have missed out on all the miracles and joy that have come along the way. Don't wait around to start living your life. If God hasn't told you NO to that person coming, then live everyday expectant that they are on the way and today could be the day. You were uniquely created to leave your MARK on this earth for Jesus. Wherever, He has placed you make the most of it. Your season could be changing soon and what an amazing day that will be.

Also remember this he or she will not fix all the things that are broken now, they cannot satisfy you fully or ever complete you, but Jesus can heal the brokenness and He is the one who fulfills us. Take this time now to find your fulfillment in Him. That way when they do come along you are less likely to place unrealistic expectations on the one He has brought to you.

You are loved. God sees every desire of your heart, so pursue His heart wholeheartedly.

Prayer:
Jesus, thank you that you are enough for me. Anything else you add unto my life is just added blessing. Thank you, Lord, that I have a significant and unique role to play in the story you are writing. Help me not to waste my days wishing my circumstances looked differently but instead live each day to the fullest knowing that you know every desire of my heart. May your will be done in my life. I trust in who you are. Amen.

TO: MY SINGLE FRIENDS

DAY 2: DID YOU HEAR GOD SAY THAT?

Genesis 2:18, 21-24

"The Lord God said, 'It is not good for the man to be alone. I will make a helper suitable for him.' So, the Lord God caused the man to fall into a deep sleep; and while he was sleeping, he took one of the man's ribs and then closed up the place with flesh. Then the Lord God made a woman from the rib he had taken out of the man, and he brought her to the man. The man said, 'This is now bone of my bones and flesh of my flesh she shall be called 'woman,' for she was taken out of man.'

That is why a man leaves his father and mother and is united to his wife, and they become one flesh".

Single Friends,

Did you hear God say to you, "_____ I am calling you to be single for the rest of your life." If you didn't hear Him say that then why are you worrying that, that's what your future holds?

In the beginning God created Adam and God saw that it wasn't good for man to be alone so what did God do? He created Eve, a helper for Adam, a companion. God values companionship between a man and a woman. He created it to be that way from the beginning. Be encouraged and grateful friends that God isn't working on our timeline. He sees the entirety of your life and He knows the exact moment your life needs to be intersected with that other person. I'm not minimizing any feelings of fear, but I can say with full confidence that you can trust and rest in God.

Singleness is just a season so don't waste this season He has entrusted to you. Use your time wisely. Create intentional community. Travel. Seek deep and true intimacy with God. Find things your passionate about. Your single season has just as much purpose and sanctification as your season of marriage, so stop looking at this season as a death sentence and make it count. We are the ones who choose whether we sulk and are miserable or whether we choose joy and live in the fullness God has for us now. Your life doesn't start when that person comes. It's happening now. Don't let it pass you by. God put His breath in your lungs today! That's a miracle! Rejoice and steward these breaths your given well.

Prayer:
Heavenly Father, thank you for speaking to me through Your Word. When the lies of the enemy come would my first reaction be to fill my mind with Your truth. Not listening to my own thoughts, or the opinions of man but instead clinging to what I know is true. Your plans for me are to prosper and not to harm, to give me hope and a future. Thank you, Jesus for that promise. Amen.

TO: MY SINGLE FRIENDS

TO: MY SINGLE FRIENDS

DAY 3: NO LIMIT

Genesis 21:1-3

*"Now the Lord was gracious to Sarah **as He had said**, and the Lord did for Sarah **what He had promised**. Sarah became pregnant and bore a son to Abraham in his old age, at the very time God had promised him. Abraham gave the name Isaac to the son Sarah bore him."*

Single Friends,

There is no age limit on your love story.

Whether you're 21 or 61+. God is able!!

He knows your heart's desire.

Don't lose heart. Don't give up.

Keep pursuing Jesus and His plan for you.

You'll meet him or her along the way.

Prayer:

Jesus, help us to remember the impossible miracles that came to pass for those who put their trust in you. Noah and the ark. Moses at the red sea. Abraham, Sarah and Issacc. Elizabeth in her old age. There are countless stories throughout your Word that speak of your perfect timing and your perfect provision. You are faithful no matter how long it may take.

We love you Jesus. May our faith grow deeper as we choose to wait on you. Amen.

TO: MY SINGLE FRIENDS

DAY 4: STOP FRANTICALLY SEARCHING

Matthew 11:29-30

"Take my yoke upon you and learn from me, for I am gentle and humble in heart, and you will find rest for your souls.

For my yoke is easy and my burden is light."

Single Friends,

What if we stopped frantically searching, wondering if he or she is the one and we asked are all knowing, all powerful God to surprise us and then trusted and believed that He actually would?

What if we fixed our eyes on Jesus, lived out His purpose for our lives and trusted that when the time is right, He would open our eyes to see and recognize the person we have been praying for. Your longings are not lost on God, nor has He forgotten your prayers.

Trust His plan for you. He will not disappoint. He will not let you down.

When the time is right, he will pursue you like God intended you to be pursued. When the time is right whoever she is will be worth pursuing with everything you have.

Follow God's lead. Rest in His peace. It's worth every bit of the wait.

Prayer:

Father, thank you that your yoke is easy, and burden is light. Teach me how to rest in your unfailing love for me, knowing that when the time is right my path will cross with the person you intended for me. I release my grip of control of my own life, my own plans and I open my hands in surrender to you. Your plans are far better, and I trust in You. Amen.

TO: MY SINGLE FRIENDS

DAY 5: FAITH

2 Corinthians 5:7

"For we live by faith, not by sight."

Proverbs 3:5-6

"Trust in the Lord with all your heart and lean not on your own understanding; in all your ways submit to him, and he will make your paths straight."

Single Friends,

Faith IS NOT a feeling!

Faith is trusting God when you can't see.

Faith is still walking forward when it doesn't look like what you thought.

Faith is pressing into Jesus when you don't feel a thing. Faith is a choice. Faith is something we have to receive from Jesus. It's not something we can muster up but something we have to ask for and open handedly receive.

Prayer:

Give us faith today Jesus so that others may see our faith and glorify YOU!

TO: MY SINGLE FRIENDS

DAY 6: NOTHING IS WASTED

James 1:2-4

"Consider it pure joy, my brothers and sisters, whenever you face trials of many kinds, because you know that the testing of your faith produces perseverance. Let perseverance finish its work so that you may be mature and complete, not lacking anything."

Single Friends,

Do you know how much Jesus loves you? Not only did He sacrifice His life on a cross for you but every single day He goes to the greatest of lengths to show you that He sees you. He sees your needs, your wants, your brokenness, your broken heart, your worry, your doubts, and your fears yet daily through a sunrise or a timely text from a friend He is reminding you that He is there, and He has not forgotten you.

I want to encourage you to take a step back and look at all the ways God is tending to your heart in the season you are in. Whether, it's big or small it shows the compassionate heart of our Father who never leaves us or forsakes us. Your circumstances might seem big, but the power and love of our God is so much bigger. He uses these mountains in our lives to strengthen our faith so that His power might be displayed in and through us to this hurting world. What an honor that God would use our circumstances and our pain as a tool for other people to see and know Him.

Let's count it all as joy friends as we face the trials of life (1) because it's shaping us to be more like Him, and (2) because it's one of the greatest ways the hope of Jesus is on display to those around us.

Our pain is never wasted with Jesus.

Prayer:

Father, thank you that not a single moment of our life is wasted when put into Your loving hands. You work all things together for the good of those who love you and are called according to your purpose. I love you Jesus. Amen.

TO: MY SINGLE FRIENDS

DAY 7: HIGH STANDARDS

2 Corinthians 9:8

"And God is able to bless you abundantly, so that in all things at all times, having all that you need, you will abound in every good work."

Single Friends,

If someone ever tells you your standards are too high remind them of who your God is!

Mountain Mover.

Sea Splitter.

Promiser of IMMEASURABLY MORE!

Don't ever settle. He is able.

Keep walking and waiting with Jesus!

Prayer:

Jesus, may I never compromise on my standards because I know that you are able exceed them. Anytime my heart grows weary in the waiting would I remember the many countless miracles you accomplished for those who walked with you years before me. You were faithful then and you will be faithful now. I trust in your unfailing love Jesus. Amen.

TO: MY SINGLE FRIENDS

DAY 8: GOD HEARS YOU

1 John 5:14-15

"This is the confidence we have in approaching God: that if we ask anything according to his will, he hears us. And if we know that he hears us—whatever we ask—we know that we have what we asked of him."

Single Friends,

As a child of God, you are GUARANTEED that when you approach the Father in prayer that He WILL hear you. Not only will He hear you but whatever you ask for in Jesus Name it shall be done unto you for His glory and for your good. He will always answer according to His will, and we can trust that His will is always what's best for us and will bring Him most glory. Approach Him with confidence. He loves you.

Prayer:

Jesus, thank you for your death and resurrection that made a way for me to approach the throne of God at any time. Thank you, Lord, that you hear me when I pray and empathize with me when I'm hurting. You are the perfect Father. Kind, compassionate and full of grace. Thank you for your love for me and making a way for me to know you. Amen.

TO: MY SINGLE FRIENDS

DAY 9: HOW TO WRESTLE WELL

2 Corinthians 4:16-18

"Therefore, we do not lose heart. Though outwardly we are wasting away, yet inwardly we are being renewed day by day. For our light and momentary troubles are achieving for us an eternal glory that far outweighs them all. So, we fix our eyes not on what is seen, but on what is unseen, since what is seen is temporary, but what is unseen is eternal."

Single Friends,

Because I share about SINGLENESS often on social media, I get asked how I walk through this season "well".

Ha-ha I don't. I wrestle. I struggle. I cry. I get mad. You have to remember that this is only social media and you are only seeing what I believe God wants me to share with you to encourage you and myself along this journey.

You don't see the countless nights I've been broken before God not understanding His timing or the moments I've cried with my closest friends and family as I've walked through heartbreak. Those are the moments that social media can't show you and we ALL have them.

If I do this whole singleness thing well, at all, it's because I've walked through deep pain and despite the pain I've run into the arms of Jesus. Sometimes, I've gone kicking and screaming but I still go. I can't express to you enough whether you're single, dating or married that it's in His presence alone that we will find all we need. Anything else is just an added bonus.

We all have a choice whether or not in those moments we run to Him or this world. There isn't an in between. What we desire as singles is not wrong. God designed us for companionship. He Himself is anticipating His own wedding one day to (us) the Bride of Christ. So, He understands the waiting, but He also knows that the wait is worth it. Just as it is and will be for you and me.

I share all of this because you aren't alone in the struggle but instead of taking matters into your own hands or settling, take it all to Jesus. Ask for His help. Sit before Him for as long as you need. He will meet you there. Don't waste this season of your life. Don't miss what God has for you today. He is good. He is your Father. He is faithful always. He will never let you down. You can trust Him and His timing. He loves you. He is for you. Speak truth over your mind and heart today. Don't let the enemy win. Take back your HOPE!

Prayer:

Thank you Jesus for the struggle. Thank you that the struggle is what draws me closer to you. It is in my weakness that your strength is displayed. Teach me how to take back my hope when the world tries to rob me of it. You are so good Father. Thank you for drawing near. Amen.

TO: MY SINGLE FRIENDS

DAY 10: REJECTION

Romans 12:9-10

"Love must be sincere. Hate what is evil; cling to what is good. Be devoted to one another in love. Honor one another above yourselves."

Single Friends,

When we are "rejected" or told no by someone may our response still be full of honor towards that person.

When we are asked out but unfortunately are not interested, may our response also be full of honor towards the person putting themselves out there.

We are brothers and sisters in Christ and our actions and words should reflect that. If we would look at rejection as God protecting us from what's not ours rather than being offended by them saying no or it not working out, we would display Christ, in a profound way, in the dating world.

Prayer:

Father, help us honor our brothers and sisters in Christ as we navigate this season of singleness and dating. You tell us in your Word to seek You in all things. May this season of our lives be no exception. Be glorified in and through us as we seek You first and then have a heart of gratitude as you add every other blessing to our life. Amen.

TO: MY SINGLE FRIENDS

DAY 11: SURRENDER

Psalm 139:13-16

*"For you created my inmost being;
you knit me together in my mother's womb.
I praise you because I am fearfully and wonderfully made;
your works are wonderful,
I know that full well.
My frame was not hidden from you
when I was made in the secret place,
when I was woven together in the depths of the earth.
Your eyes saw my unformed body;
all the days ordained for me were written in your book
before one of them came to be."*

Single Friends,

God ordained all of your days before even one came to be. He saw it all before you were even born. So whatever it is you are worried about right now, surrender it to Jesus. If He already sees all your days you can trust that He is leading you to His best for you even when life doesn't make much sense. He is good. Trust. Trust. Trust in Him.

Prayer:

Jesus, I am choosing to put my trust in You today. I trust Your plans, not my own. I trust your timing, not the timing I think is best. Help me to be thankful for the people and blessings you have placed in my life right now. Amen.

TO: MY SINGLE FRIENDS

DAY 12: WAITING WELL

Isaiah 40:30-31

"Even youths shall faint and be weary, and young men shall fall exhausted;

but they who wait for the Lord shall renew their strength; they shall mount up with wings like eagles;

they shall run and not be weary; they shall walk and not faint."

Single Friends,

One of my constant prayers is that God would use my life and testimony to encourage a generation of women and men who will expectantly WAIT on God's timing. He writes the very best stories. Stories way better than any of us could ever write ourselves. I read this poem in my *Streams in the Desert* devotional my sweet Grandmama gave me and its one worth sharing.

"Waiting! Yes, patiently waiting!
Till next steps made plain shall be;
To hear, with inner hearing,
The Voice that will call for me.
Waiting! Yes, hopefully waiting!
With hope that need not grow dim;
The Master is pledged to guide me,
And my eyes are unto Him.
Waiting! Expectantly waiting!
Perhaps it may be today
The Master will quickly open
The gate to my future way.
Waiting! Yes, waiting! Still waiting! I know,
though I've waited long, That, while He withholds His purpose,
His waiting cannot be wrong.
Waiting! Yes, waiting! Still waiting! The Master will not be late: He knoweth that I am waiting
for Him to unlatch the gate." - J Danson Smith.

Prayer:
Jesus, thank you that waiting on you is never in vain. My season of waiting on you is cultivating a deep trust in The One that already knows my future. Thank you Jesus for giving me the strength to wait on your timing and trust in your plan. Be near Lord. I need you. Amen.

TO: MY SINGLE FRIENDS

DAY 13: THIS IS LOVE

Single Friends,

Don't buy into the worlds view of love. Love isn't someone's outward appearance. Love isn't found in someone's status or their amount of followers. Love isn't lust. Love is not even based off of our feelings because our feelings are fickle moment to moment and day to day. Love is not momentary satisfaction. Love isn't what the media shows us in the movies and in porn. The worlds love is shallow and displays nothing but a false and distorted version of what God intended love to be.

This is love... *"Love is patient, love is kind. It does not envy, it does not boast, it is not proud. It does not dishonor others, it is not self-seeking, it is not easily angered, it keeps no record of wrongs. Love does not delight in evil but rejoices with the truth. It always protects, always trusts, always hopes, always perseveres. Love never fails."* - **1 Corinthians 13:4-8**

God's love and the love He intends for you to experience in a companion is completely counter cultural to this world. Fight for and wait on the person God has chosen to love you, for who you are and the season you are in. In the waiting God will sustain you and as you wait, seek His love. It really is the only love that will ever satisfy. You are enough and God is not finished writing your story. Choose the kind of love that's eternal and makes a difference for His Kingdom. That's the love we were all created for.

Prayer:

You are love, Jesus. As I pursue you more would I learn more about what love really is and how to love those around me like you love them. May my life be counter cultural to this world and be a display of who you are. Amen.

TO: MY SINGLE FRIENDS

DAY 14: KNOW YOUR WORTH

Romans 12:2

"Do not conform to the pattern of this world, but be transformed by the renewing of your mind. Then you will be able to test and approve what God's will is—his good, pleasing and perfect will."

Single Friends,

Is the person you are talking to seeking to be more like Christ? Are they seeking older wisdom and discipleship? Are they pursuing you as a daughter or a son of God or is the pursuit a lustful one? If they aren't willing to commit to a Christ centered pursuit of your heart and Gods it's only right for you to assume that their pursuit is self-centered and it is probably time to say goodbye!

Know your worth!

Prayer:

Father, transform my mind. May I seek and desire the things of heaven and not the things of this world. Give me the strength to wait on someone who is so in love with you and will pursue my heart like you always intended them to. Your plans are better than mine. Give me strength in the waiting.
Amen.

TO: MY SINGLE FRIENDS

DAY 15: IN SECONDS

Proverbs 3:5-6

"Trust in the Lord with all your heart

and lean not on your own understanding;

in all your ways submit to him,

and he will make your paths straight."

Single Friends,

One afternoon I put a bouquet of flowers that had not yet bloomed in a vase with some water. Later, that evening I had gone downstairs to take my puppy outside and the flowers that were just buds earlier that day had begun to bloom.

How kind God is that through a bouquet of flowers He would remind me that the circumstances of my life and yours can change within a matter of seconds, hours, or even just a day. We can hold onto the hope that our Jesus hears our prayers and holds them in His hands. So don't give up.

He also reminded me through a sermon that even when we are obedient to Him and our circumstances don't change that He, God, The Creator of the Universe is still WITH ME and He is WITH YOU and HE LOVES US SO MUCH. He is always there for us and that is a promise we can hold onto when everything else is shaken. Praying we all find rest in the power, love and sovereignty of our Almighty, Loving Heavenly Father who sees us and knows exactly what we need when we need it.

Prayer:

Jesus, what an amazing thought that the circumstances of my life can change in seconds. Teach me how to wait expectantly for the things you have in store and to trust in you with my whole heart. I may not understand your timing but I can cling to the promise that you are always with me and will never forsake me. You are enough for me Jesus. I love you. Amen.

TO: MY SINGLE FRIENDS

DAY 16: YES, LORD

Matthew 9:27-30

"As Jesus went on from there, two blind men followed Him, calling out, 'Have mercy on us, Son of David!' When He had gone indoors, the blind men came to Him, and He asked them, 'Do you believe that I am able to do this?' 'Yes, Lord,' they replied. Then he touched their eyes and said, 'According to your faith let it be done to you'; and their sight was restored. Jesus warned them sternly, 'See that no one knows about this.' "

Single Friends,

Maybe all Jesus wants from us is a "Yes Lord" when He asks us if we believe He is able. It's not about what we do for Him but about simple childlike faith. Good gifts from God are simply received because of His unmatched grace not by anything you or I do. Stop striving and keep believing. We live by faith, not by sight.

Prayer:

Father, I repent of my striving. I want to live with childlike faith. Develop in me a trust so deep in you that I don't worry about what tomorrow holds but instead rest in the grace you have for me today. Yes, Lord, I believe you are able. Amen.

TO: MY SINGLE FRIENDS

DAY 17: CHASE YOUR DREAMS

Acts 20:24

However, I consider my life worth nothing to me; my only aim is to finish the race and complete the task the Lord Jesus has given me—the task of testifying to the good news of God's grace.

Single Friends,

It's so easy to want to wait for your special person to be in your life before you chase your dreams, but reality is we aren't promised tomorrow. Go after your dreams now. Run your race well. You will run into them on the journey and can finish running your races together.

Run well for the "well done" from God.

Run well for the eternities that are on the line.

Oh man it's going to be so worth it!! Enjoy the in between.

Prayer:

Jesus, thank you for the breath in my lungs today. Give me fresh sight to see what you are doing all around me. Help me to not allow my desire for a relationship to rob me of what you desire to do through me in this season. Show me how to run my race well, Lord. You are worthy. Amen.

TO: MY SINGLE FRIENDS

DAY 18: "IF __ HAPPENS.."

Psalm 55:22

*"Cast your cares on the Lord
and he will sustain you;
he will never let
the righteous be shaken."*

Single Friends,

Anyone else tell God… "If _____ happens I won't be able to handle it or I won't be able to make it."

A lot of those "If _____ Happens," statements that I've made to God throughout my life have come to pass in the last year or so. I'm still in the midst of most of them and it's hard.

But I'm here to tell you that God will not leave you and He will sustain you one minute and one day at a time. Whatever you're walking through that you don't believe you can handle, you can because God is by your side. God is fighting your battles. God loves you with a never ending love. You'll make it and your faith will be stronger because of it. I promise. Whatever it is that you're walking through, don't walk through it alone. Get involved in a local church. Confide in someone you trust. Spend time in the presence of God and in His Word. He will meet you exactly where you are.

Prayer:
Thank you for sustaining me in all seasons Jesus. Lead me to the places where I can find community that will point me towards You when things don't make sense. Even in the midst of the unknown I will choose to run to You and rest in knowing that You see the bigger picture. Amen.

TO: MY SINGLE FRIENDS

DAY 19: UNSHAKEABLE FAITH

1 Corinthians 15:58

"Therefore, my dear brothers and sisters, stand firm. Let nothing move you. Always give yourselves fully to the work of the Lord, because you know that your labor in the Lord is not in vain."

Single Friends,

"When sight ceases, it is the time for faith to work. The greater the difficulties, the easier it is for faith. As long as human possibilities for success remain, faith does not accomplish things as easily as when all natural prospects fail. - George Mueller, *The Autobiography of George Muller*

FAITH is something God has been teaching me a lot about. Not a happy go lucky, make you feel good kind of faith, but the kind of faith you need when you're on the verge of giving up or completely throwing in the towel. A faith you can cling to when everything you thought you heard from God isn't matching up with what you're seeing right in front of you.

All faith has to be tested though, because if it isn't then our faith doesn't grow and God intended for our faith to grow deep. Deep enough that when the storms of life come (because they will) we aren't immediately uprooted but instead stand firm. Believing and trusting God is hard especially in seasons of pain but when we look throughout scripture these seasons of pain reap the greatest harvest. So hold on to hope friends. Hold on to Jesus. He's not ever going to let you down. He's refining you and the refinement is worth it.

Prayer:

Lord, if it's through seasons of pain that I grow the most than would you give me the strength to stand firm as I walk through it. You are my firm foundation.

TO: MY SINGLE FRIENDS

DAY 20: SETTLING? NO WAY!

Single Friends,

Whoever told you, you had to lower your standards or that you had to settle? Was it your family? Maybe your friends? Maybe it was even the time that's passing? Or possibly your circumstances made you convinced that was the only option?

I want to encourage you ~ if I know anything about God, from reading scripture, it's that He is a God of MORE. A God that exceeds our wildest dreams. He is a God who gives abundantly to His children, and if that is who He is than He would never tell you to settle or to lower any standard. Instead to set the bar high because of who He is!

He is the one who gives us the strength to pursue patience, wisdom, and self-control. He is the one who moves mountains and splits seas.

As a child of God you deserve to be pursued FAITHFULLY AND INTENTIONALLY. Nothing less. Is that guy or girl going to be perfect? Well no because only Jesus holds that title, but you can believe that if God went to great lengths so you could live free and abundantly then why would He not extend that same abundance into your relationships.

In a world that is chasing after something immediate and settling for less let's press into God and wait on His very best. I'm not saying not to date because I think it's good when done intentionally and when God is included in the conversation. Just like you reach out to God for direction for a job, He delights when you seek Him about something as important as a potential spouse.

Pursue Jesus. Ask Him what healthy expectations are. Seek His wisdom and His standards for you as His child. Listen. Write them down and then hold fast to what He says. He is the one who lights our path and that path always leads to more joy if we let Him lead.

In the meantime, in the waiting, pursue God with all your heart and pray that whoever he or she is, is seeking Him wholeheartedly to.

Prayer:
Jesus, may your will be done in my life and my future spouses life. Lead my every step and lead theirs. May both of our lives be in complete surrender to you.

TO: MY SINGLE FRIENDS

DAY 21: WAITING ON HIM

John 1:5

"The light shines in the darkness, and the darkness has not overcome it."

Single Friends,

When you choose to really walk with God and wait on Him there will be people who won't understand. There will be people you love who will say things that they think will comfort you but actually hurt you. You will have days where you want to throw in the towel, to settle for less and to tell God you can do His job better. There will be moments so painfully crushing that you think that you won't make it to the next day.

Yet, in the midst of it all God makes His way into the darkness you're walking through with His light. His light brings us tremendous hope and it expels the darkness. His light reminds us the tunnel will soon end. His light helps us make our way out of the valley onto the mountaintop. You may feel like your fire has burnt out in this season, but I'm here to remind you like God has reminded me that our light doesn't dwindle when we walk through hard seasons. Hard seasons are when people see His light the most. Let His light shine dear friend. No striving. Just being. Just resting that when God says His plan is to prosper you and not harm you that He means it. Let this season of refining complete its work so you can shine bright for Him forevermore. He has not forsaken you and He never will.

Extra tip: be honest and vulnerable with those around you about the season you're walking through. Let them love you, walk with you and pray for you. God created us to walk in authenticity with others not like we have it all together all the time. It's okay to not be okay.

Prayer:

Lord, thank you for being light in some of my darkest nights. It's your light that has sustained me. May that same light shine bright through me to those around me so that they might find the same hope in their darkest night.

TO: MY SINGLE FRIENDS

DAY 22: IMMEASURABLY MORE

Ephesians 3:20-21

"Now to him who is able to do immeasurably more than all we ask or imagine, according to his power that is at work within us, to him be glory in the church and in Christ Jesus throughout all generations, for ever and ever! Amen.

Single Friends,

"Why settle for less when you serve the God of immeasurably more?"

He is able to make that impossible dream possible. He is able to bring you everything your heart desires in a future spouse. He is able to bring healing to your body. He is able to mend your broken family and to free you from that addiction. He is able to do ALL things, we just have to start believing Him.

Prayer:

Jesus, let faith arise in me and every doubt be silenced in Your Name. I believe You are able and willing to do all things but help me with my unbelief. You are a miracle worker and a promise keeper. I love you. I am choosing today to put my hope, my trust and my faith in who You are.
Amen

TO: MY SINGLE FRIENDS

DAY 23: DISTRACTION

Hebrews 12:1-3

Therefore, since we are surrounded by such a great cloud of witnesses, let us throw off everything that hinders and the sin that so easily entangles. And let us run with perseverance the race marked out for us, fixing our eyes on Jesus, the pioneer and perfecter of faith. For the joy set before him he endured the cross, scorning its shame, and sat down at the right hand of the throne of God. Consider him who endured such opposition from sinners, so that you will not grow weary and lose heart.

Single Friends,

What the enemy can't defeat, he distracts! Be aware of the things that he may be using to take your attention off of the things that matter most. Ask God to shine a light on those places of distraction and ask Him for His help to keep you focused on running your race well. Life is but a breath. Let's not waste it.

Prayer:

Jesus, I'm fixing my eyes on you. Not looking to the left or right but focusing on you and the race you have set before me. Keep my life free from distraction and show me the places that are distractions that I may not recognize. You are my everything Lord. I love you. Amen

TO: MY SINGLE FRIENDS

DAY 24: BELIEVE

James 4:2

"You do not have because you do not ask God."

Single Friends,

It's okay to believe for your miracle with a broken heart.

God knows. God sees. He will be faithful. Just don't lose heart.

Prayer:

Jesus, I bring all the broken pieces of my heart to you. I'm laying all the disappointment and pain down at your feet and I am choosing to believe for a miracle. You say in your Word that I don't have because I don't ask so I am asking in faith that you would bring that person into my life in accordance to Your will not my own. I believe You are able. Amen.

TO: MY SINGLE FRIENDS

DAY 25: NO QUICK MIRACLES

Galatians 5:22-23

"But the fruit of the Spirit is love, joy, peace, patience, kindness, goodness, faithfulness, gentleness, self-control; against such things there is no law."

Single Friends,

Someone needs to be reminded that the God who will bring the MIRACLE ENDING to your story is the same God who is with you when you feel like settling. We all give up too easy. We all want a quick fix. None of us want to wait. I don't know of many stories in the Bible where God did "quick" miracles. There are always seasons of waiting, seasons of wilderness, seasons of being in The Refiners fire. There have been hours, days, and months of doubt and questioning God. Questioning His timing and His plan. Even getting in the way of His plan. That's why His Word has to be our source. It's the days when I'm away from His Word that I doubt the most. When I wonder if He is able and He will do what I know He is able to do.

I didn't date for 7 years and not dating for that long was THE HARDEST thing I've ever done, because it was the one thing I didn't want to give up. It was the one thing that kept me from experiencing all that Jesus had for me because I placed my value in men instead of in Him. I would not trade those years of refinement for anything. Those years have deepened my love and dependence on Jesus. Those years are equipping me to be the wife that He will call me to be one day. In the end the waiting is ridding me of myself and producing in me more of my Savior and for that I'm grateful.

Friends, don't just date to date. Ask God for clarity. Wait on God. Ask for His strength. Find accountability. Surrender and continue to run your race. One day you'll run into each other, begin to run this race together and it will all be worth it.

Prayer:

Lord, thank you for every season and for the lessons you are teaching me in each one. Open my eyes to see the beauty that's all around me in my season of singleness. I don't want to miss out on what you're doing and where you're leading. You are good. Amen.

TO: MY SINGLE FRIENDS

DAY 26: COMMUNITY MATTERS

Single Friends,

If you've been lonely and are praying for community and still haven't found it, don't give up. Keep praying and putting yourself out there. God asks us to wait on Him, but He also says to walk with Him too. You don't have to go frantically searching for community but God does require us to take some steps of faith.

Sign up to serve, send a text to that person you met and grab dinner. YOU plan a group hangout. Sometimes the way we find community is by creating it our self and being the one to invite others in.

Sure it's easy to just sit at home, watch tv, and not go to that event. When we do that we are missing out on the gift of friendship that God created for us to enjoy. You may feel awkward at first but I can promise you that the treasure you will find in the people God places in your life are worth pushing through those feelings for. God created us to walk with one another. Don't walk this journey alone. Maybe the answer to your prayers is on the other side of you taking that one step. Be strong and courageous. Confident in who God made you to be. Praying tonight whoever you are that God will whisper your next step to you for you to find the people He desires you to walk with. The people He created to encourage you and you them. Friends who will challenge you, keep you accountable, and run this race of faith alongside you. God hears your prayers. He loves you. If you've been praying for this for awhile and have seen no results maybe it's your time to make a move. If you've just started praying, keep praying and trusting and stepping. God will meet you there.

Prayer:

Father, would you show me the next step I need to take to find the community you desire for me to have. Help me to step out of my comfort zone and partner with you in finding the friends I have always prayed for. Thank you Jesus that through every friend we will learn more about who you are since we are all made in Your image. Lead my steps they are surrendered to You. Amen.

TO: MY SINGLE FRIENDS

DAY 27: LET'S BE HONEST

Job 17:11-12

"My days have passed, my plans are shattered. Yet the desires of my heart turn night into day; in the face of darkness light is near."

Single Friends,

Job was so honest with God in the midst of his pain. God invites you and I into His presence when we are broken, messy and afraid of the unknown. What's so beautiful about these scriptures is that Job recognizes his circumstances are dark, but he knows in the midst of any darkness that LIGHT is near. God is near to you in your darkest seasons. He has brought His light to illuminate every fear, every doubt and fill you up with fresh hope.

We all walk through seasons of pain. You are not alone and don't forget that this season won't be wasted.

Prayer:

Lord, thank you that Your light is always near in the darkest nights. Thank you for walking with me through every season and every step. You will never leave me or forsake me. I am so thankful for Your promises. Amen.

TO: MY SINGLE FRIENDS

DAY 28: HOW MUCH MORE

Matthew 7:11

"If you, then, though you are evil, know how to give good gifts to your children, how much more will your Father in heaven give good gifts to those who ask him!"

Outside of saying yes to a relationship with Jesus I don't know that there is a more important decision any of us will make than choosing who we say yes to spending the rest of our life with. I also believe that it's a decision God wants to weigh in on. It says in Psalm 139:16 that He ordained all our days before even one came to be so why would we not seek the counsel of The One who has already seen all of our days?

I am still single, choosing to wait on God and asking for discernment every step of the way. I'd be lying to you though if I didn't say that it's hard. To think about settling and missing out on Gods best is harder though.

Watching those around me settle because they are tired of waiting is painful. Seeing those around me frantically searching is heartbreaking. What happened to trusting in the Lord with all our heart? When we put our trust in Him there is no need for panic. When we know the character of our Father there is no need to be afraid. He says in Matthew 7 that if you who are evil know how to give good gifts to your children than HOW MUCH MORE will your HEAVENLY FATHER give good gifts to those who ask Him. How many of us have asked God to guide us as we date? How many of us have asked for strength to continue to wait? How many of us are asking God to align our path with our husband or wife? (He didn't say you can't ask, He said TO ask.) Are we asking God to be in these decisions with us, or do we think we can handle it better on our own? From my own personal experience doing it on my own led me to more sin, more heartbreak, more of self and less of Jesus. I don't think I'm alone in that either. We can't navigate this life without Him and life with Him is so much more abundant. God has someone in mind for you. In this season instead of frantically searching keep growing. Grow in your faith. Become the kind of person you are praying for. Walk away from that relationship you know in your heart isn't meant for you. Let God heal you and ready you for who He has in mind. The love stories God writes are ones that don't only benefit you but benefit those around you for His glory. Its worth the wait!

Prayer:
Jesus, give me patience in the waiting and strength not to settle. Waiting on you will always reap the greatest story. Amen.

DAY 29: WHAT I'VE LEARNED

Single Friends,

I'm praying that some of the things God has taught me from dating and waiting will encourage you as you learn to wait on God and date intentionally with eternity in mind not just momentary satisfaction.

1. If someone asks you out and you aren't interested don't say yes and go on a pity date. It doesn't honor them. Just say NO.

2. If you know it isn't right don't ghost them, or text them you are no longer interested, be mature and call them.

3. Don't be afraid to ask questions that are important to you upfront. If they are scared away by them then they aren't the one for you.

4. Know your non-negotiable's and don't settle. God is not going to send you someone who will "just work." He will bring someone into your life who you can run your race well with. They may not have the exact same calling as you but they will champion you in yours and you will be excited to champion them in theirs.

5. Don't keep dating someone longer out of fear of their reaction. Be honest. You don't want to waste their time or yours.

6. GUARD YOUR HEART! God doesn't say guard their heart He says to guard YOURS. Only they can guard their own heart, that's not your responsibility. Honor, honor, honor them though.

7. Don't date frantically out of fear of being alone. Date intentionally. Date PRAYERFULLY. God is our best friend and the best mentor any of us could ever seek out advice or guidance from. He will always lead you to His best and perfect will for your life. Trust Him. Rest in Him. Seek His face. The rest will fall into place.

8. Don't wait until you meet your spouse to start praying for them. Create a habit of praying intentionally for them now. Prayer matters. Prayer moves the heart of God. …. above all remember this, whether you are single, dating or waiting, Jesus loves you and your life matters so much to Him. He is our first love and before He gives us the gift of companionship here on earth let's make sure we are standing firm in our identity as beloved sons and daughters of Jesus. No earthly love will ever satisfy us like His love.

TO: MY SINGLE FRIENDS

DAY 30: I'LL WAIT DECLARATION

A Declaration of Surrender to Jesus

Because I belong to Jesus and He is my first love I will -

I will seek first His Kingdom
I will wait on His leading
I will trust in His timing
I will pursue purity
I will flee from temptation
I will love without condition
I will seek out accountability
I will plant myself in God's Word
I will date with intentionality and not passivity
I will not settle but instead wait expectantly for His best
I will honor my brothers and sisters in Christ
I will use my tongue to speak life and not death
I will choose to believe and not doubt
I will run my race well in every season
I will boldly proclaim The Gospel
I will live in His peace and rebuke fear
I will choose hope
I will not despair
I will be a light in the darkness
I will live by faith and not by sight
I will rejoice in hope
I will be patient in affliction
I will be faithful in prayer
I will be still and know He is God
I will receive His daily grace
I will surrender my plans
I will trust in Him always

I will wait on you Lord.

TO: MY SINGLE FRIENDS

A PRAYER FOR THE HOLIDAYS

Single Friends,

You are on God's radar always but especially in this season.
Here is my prayer for you and I as we walk through each holiday.

Father,
I thank you for meeting us right where we are. You go before us and behind us. You know our every need and our every want and because you are our Father you know what's best for us. Your timing is always good.

Jesus right now I pray you would pour out an extra measure of your grace, mercy, joy, hope and love over all of us who are in a season of singleness. You are enough Lord, but you do not ever dismiss our pain. Help us to bring every tear, every question, every angry thought to your feet. May we not run away from you Jesus, but may we be found running to you where we can find all we need.

Father will you protect us from words that are spoken that aren't from you? Will you help us to give grace to our family members during these days? Give us supernatural strength and JOY. Help us to see YOU all around us. Give us hearts of thankfulness for this season.

Open our eyes God to see family members who need encouragement and your love.
God thank you for being full of kindness and compassion.
It is your joy to answer our prayers and give us the desires of our hearts in accordance to your will and timing.

May we wait in HOPEFUL EXPECTATION and ANTICIPATION for all that you have in store for us.
Mold us into who you've called us to be in the in between. May you protect us from every scheme of the enemy and remind us each morning to put our armor on.
You have always been and will forever be faithful. May our hearts know that in full tonight and forevermore.

We love you Jesus and we trust you. Amen!

Take some time tonight just writing out all the things your thankful for. From the breath in your lungs to the new promotion you just got. It's all from God. Seeing it all written out may just be what you need to help change your perspective.

You are not alone.

TO: MY SINGLE FRIENDS

TWO OPTIONS

Psalm 86:4

"Bring joy to your servant, Lord, for I put my trust in you."

Single Friends,

You and I have 2 options this holiday season. We either let the enemy steal our joy OR we ask God to help us see the gift this season is and choose joy.

Choosing the latter is the better option. We give the enemy far too much power in our lives. He doesn't get to steal our joy unless we allow him to.

Please don't think I am minimizing the pain and hurt you may be experiencing as you walk through this season. It is real and your pain is not lost on God. He is very familiar with it.

What if we turned our thoughts around? What if we were expectant that God was going to do something new in this season? What if we chose to be present with our families and gave thanks to God for the gifts He has given to us instead of dwelling on the things that have yet to come?

I believe that as we set our gaze on Jesus, when we ask Him for His help, He delights in that and will answer.

He will give you joy if you ask.

He will be your strength if you let Him. He is able to fill you up to overflowing even in the seasons where you feel you are lacking.

He cares about the desires of your heart. He is still writing your story, but in the meantime don't miss what He has for you in this chapter.

You are seen. You are loved. You are chosen by the Greatest Love of All.

TO: MY SINGLE FRIENDS

ANOTHER SINGLE HOLIDAY

Single Friends,

I know. I know. Here comes this time of year again and you said to yourself this time last year something along the lines of "surely this next year God will bring them into my life", or you prayed a prayer like this one - "God please don't make me spend another holiday season in this season of singleness."

I want to remind you that it's okay to grieve your hearts desire not being fulfilled yet. Its alright to tell God how you really feel. He already knows anyway. Speaking it out into the light helps bitterness not take root in our hearts towards God or this season in our lives. Take all the pain to Jesus and ask Him to give you the strength to keep waiting, not to settle, and to open your eyes to all the amazing things He wants to do in and through you right where you are.

God IS NOT withholding anything good from you in this season. He knows the right time that man or woman is suppose to enter your life. Don't allow the enemy to make you question Gods character or make you question your worth. Your value isn't based on your relationship status. Your worth is rooted in being a child of God and the Bride of Christ. I know family can be hard around the holidays. Always asking the wrong questions with the best intentions. So ask God before every gathering to help you guard your heart and to show them grace. Don't let your longing rob you of the precious memories you have with those who love you most.

I wish I could sit with each of you reading this and tell you face to face that GOD HAS NOT FORSAKEN YOU. Every prayer you've ever prayed in this area has not and will not ever be forgotten by God. He knows you better than you know you. Right now He is building in you an unshakeable trust and faith in Him and there is nothing more valuable then the things God wants to produce in us. So persevere. Hold tight to your faith. Pursue the heart of Christ with all you've got. Wait expectantly for our faithful Jesus to go above and beyond all you can ask for or imagine. Pray intentionally for that person you're believing for and keep becoming all God intended you to be. Jesus loves you and you matter so much to Him.

TO: MY SINGLE FRIENDS

TIS THE SEASON

Hebrews 11:1

"Now faith is confidence in what we hope for and assurance about what we do not see."

Isaiah 58:11

"The LORD will guide you always; He will satisfy your needs in a sun-scorched land and will strengthen your frame. You will be like a well-watered garden, like a spring whose waters never fail."

Single Friends,

The holidays can be hard especially with all the questions from loved ones and just the reality that you may be the only one without a special someone.

I just wanted to take a second to remind you and myself - that you are not less than because of the season you're in. Singleness is just as much a gift as being in a relationship. Unfortunately our world has fed us the lie that it is a curse. Don't allow that lie to make you forget the truth, that you have so much purpose and so much to give right where you are.

Ask God to show you how to love and serve those around you best this season. It's so easy to allow the longing of a future relationship steal away the joy of what's right in front of you. Celebrate your family, friends and our Savior.

Having our focus upward on Jesus and outward on others keeps us from dwelling too much on our lack and reminds us of the abundance we have in Christ.

He is writing a beautiful story friend. Keep entrusting Him with your life. He will never let you down.

TO: MY SINGLE FRIENDS

ABOUT THE AUTHOR

Allie Shirley is an established entrepreneur, speaker, author, with a passion for Jesus and people. She has owned her online clothing company Marqué Made for 6 years and is expanding globally to help provide jobs for women who are at risk or have been rescued from human trafficking in America, Thailand and Moldova. Faith, singleness and justice are just a few of the things she is passionate about. Allie has shared her story of hope on college campuses, in small group settings and on stages in the north and south east. Her greatest heart's desire is for people all over the world to know that Jesus loves them and that they matter.

Connect with Allie on Facebook and Instagram.
Personal Instagram: @missmarquemade
Book Instagram: @tomysinglefriends

Email us! We would love to hear from you: tomysinglefriends@gmail.com

TO: MY SINGLE FRIENDS

Made in the USA
Coppell, TX
26 December 2019